An Edible Alphabet

26 Reasons to Love the Farm

by Carol Watterson

Illustrated by Michela Sorrentino

TRICYCLE PRESS
Berkeley

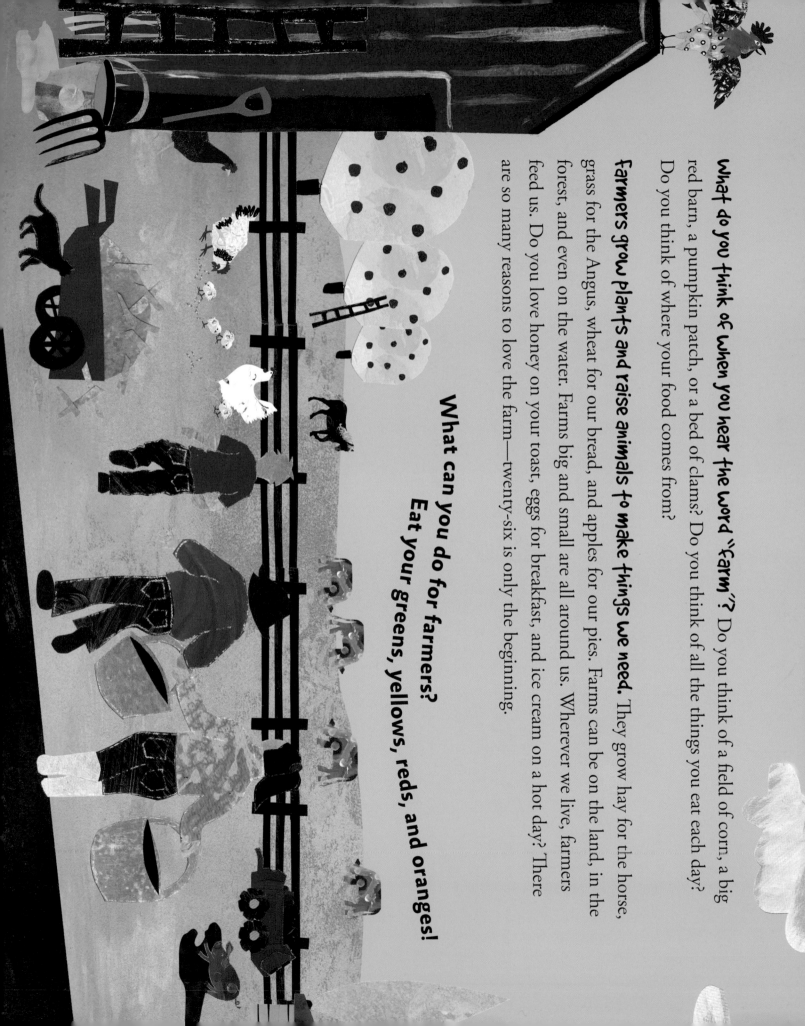

What do you think of when you hear the word "farm"? Do you think of a field of corn, a big red barn, a pumpkin patch, or a bed of clams? Do you think of all the things you eat each day? Do you think of where your food comes from?

Farmers grow plants and raise animals to make things we need. They grow hay for the horse, grass for the Angus, wheat for our bread, and apples for our pies. Farms can be on the land, in the forest, and even on the water. Farms big and small are all around us. Wherever we live, farmers feed us. Do you love honey on your toast, eggs for breakfast, and ice cream on a hot day? There are so many reasons to love the farm—twenty-six is only the beginning.

What can you do for farmers?
Eat your greens, yellows, reds, and oranges!

Let's turn the page to find a farmyard feast from A to Z . . .

Aa

Ants on Asparagus

Who are those little green soldiers poking their heads through the brown earth? Asparagus! Spring's first arrivals on the farm! One, two, three— let's count the knobby crowns reaching for the sun while ants tickle their tender stalks.

Many crops, like wheat and corn, grow from seeds the farmer plants each spring. Asparagus is different; it doesn't need to be planted every spring. Each season the farmer harvests only the stalk, and leaves the roots in the soil. Next spring, the plant will grow new shoots from its roots.

Ants are insect farmers. Aphids make a sweet, sticky substance called honeydew that the ants harvest for food. Ants will herd their aphids like cattle, carrying them to new food sources. The ants protect their aphid herd from predators, such as ladybugs and asparagus beetles. Ants will even save the aphid eggs in their ant nests over the winter and then bring their new herd out in the spring.

The ants go marching up and down the asparagus, hunting for aphids.

Bb

Blueberries,
Beets, and Beans

Blueberries bounce, brown beans jump,

and green beans bend.

A farmer grows a rainbow. Red radishes, orange carrots, and purple beets hide in the soil waiting to be picked. Black, pink, and speckled beans jump out of their green jackets to show off their colors. Green Bartlett pears turn bright yellow when they're ripe and ready to eat. Fill your plate with lots of different colors—it's good for you!

Fruits such as blueberries and blackberries have colorful names. Can you think of other foods that have colorful names?

It's a bucketful of color!

Cc

Clip, Clop, Crunch

Carrots are a crunchy treat, but horses also munch on alfalfa hay, grass, and oats. Apples too!

Did you know that not all carrots are orange? Some varieties are red, yellow, purple, and even white.

Sneak a peek on the next page to see how carrots grow . . . .

Dd

Dig in for Dinner

Look down. Vegetables are hiding in the deep, dark soil.

What vegetables can you find growing underground?

Something magical is happening down below. Root vegetables are drawing nutrients from the soil and slowly developing from tiny seeds into bumpy globes and cone-shaped wonders. Dig down, dig around, then grab a leafy top and give it a good yank. **PoP! out comes dinner.**

Potatoes belong to a group of vegetables called tubers. The part we eat is the round, underground stem. While potatoes can be grown from seeds of the plant's flowers, most are grown from other potatoes called seed potatoes.

A plant sprouts from the seed-potato's eyes— those little nubby bits. Leafy tops reach for the sky while the roots dig deep into the earth. There, in the darkness, an underground stem grows and the potatoes (*tubers*) develop. When the plant is in full flower, your potatoes are ready to harvest. Time to roll up your sleeves and get digging!

Potatoes have a funny nickname: spuds. How do you like to eat your spuds?

Ee

Eager Ewes

Everywhere the ewes go, the lambs are sure to follow.

Five Fleecy Facts

1. **Sheep do not like to be alone.** They flock together in groups and have a strong instinct to follow their leader. If the lead ram jumps over a stick, and the stick is taken away, the other sheep will still jump over the spot where the stick was!

2. **Sheep eat grass and grain** and are called *ruminants*. This means they have four parts to their stomach. These are like storage places that help digest the tough hay and grasses that sheep graze on.

3. **Sheep provide us with many useful things,** like wool, meat, sheepskin, milk, and cheese. Fat from sheep, called *tallow*, is used to make candles and soap.

4. **Female sheep are called ewes** and male sheep are called *rams*.

5. **Sheep have an excellent sense of smell.** That's because they have scent glands in front of their eyes as well as on their feet. Can you smell with your toes?

Ff

Flip Flop Fry

See the flashes of silver fins on the water?
It's young salmon fry swimming up the river.

Wild salmon live in both fresh- and saltwater during different stages of their life cycle. They are born in rivers, where they spend the first part of their lives as tiny fish called *alevin* before growing into young *fry*. After a couple of years spent feeding and growing, the fry gather together and make their way toward the open water. Adult salmon live in the ocean for three or four years before returning to their home river to spawn and lay their own eggs for the next generation.

If too many salmon are fished from the oceans, not enough will remain to return to their rivers to spawn and reproduce. Wild salmon is a precious resource—not just for us, but for wildlife species such as bears, seals, and eagles that rely upon it for their food.

There are many different ways to harvest fish.

Some methods are healthy for the ocean's ecosystem, while others are not. Some commercial fishing boats, called trawlers, use long poles with lines and bait that only catch one fish at a time. This way of fishing does not accidentally catch marine mammals, sea turtles, seabirds, or endangered fish the way nets do.

We can help protect life in our oceans by choosing to eat seafood that has been caught or raised using methods that are more environmentally responsible.

Gg

Gaggle of Giggling Geese

Geese don't really giggle. They honk. When they are mad, they hiss.

A goose says "hello" with a honk. More than one honk usually means trouble. That's why geese make good guards on the farm. Loud honking is useful when predators, such as raccoons or foxes, sneak into the barnyard. Can you honk like a goose?

Geese are great lawnmowers. A goose's bill is shaped like a triangle, and instead of teeth, it has sharp notches along its edges. These notches are good for cutting through dry grass and short plants, which geese love to eat. Geese eat weeds, but not crops, and this makes the farmer happy. After a grassy meal, geese sometimes splash and frolic in the water. *This might even make them giggle.*

A goose, a gander, and some goslings— together they're called a gaggle.

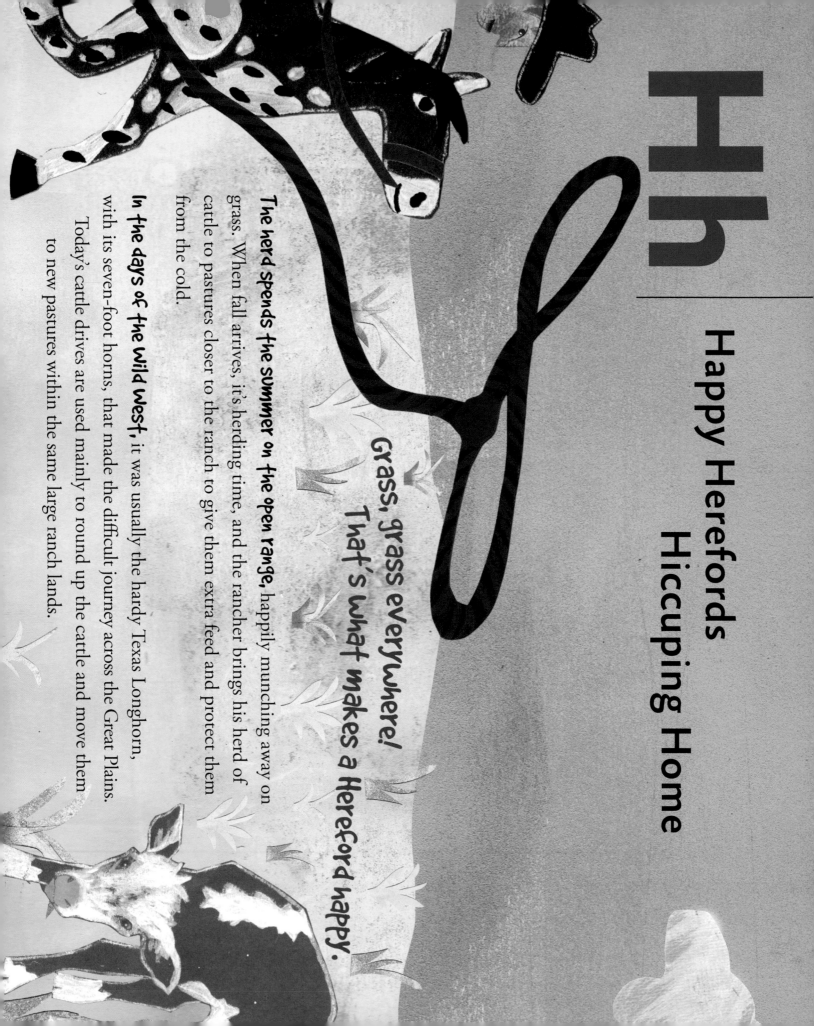

Hh

Happy Herefords
Hiccuping Home

Grass, grass everywhere!
That's what makes a Hereford happy.

The herd spends the summer on the open range, happily munching away on grass. When fall arrives, it's herding time, and the rancher brings his herd of cattle to pastures closer to the ranch to give them extra feed and protect them from the cold.

In the days of the wild west, it was usually the hardy Texas Longhorn, with its seven-foot horns, that made the difficult journey across the Great Plains. Today's cattle drives are used mainly to round up the cattle and move them to new pastures within the same large ranch lands.

A cow spends all day eating and chewing her cud. That's because, like a sheep, she's a ruminant. While most animals have only one stomach to fill, ruminants have four parts to their stomach. Food is stored in one part called the *rumen*. When the rumen is full, the cow lies down, hiccups up portions of food, rechews and reswallows, sending it to the other three stomachs to be digested.

Only a mother cow should be called a cow. The youngsters are called *calves* and the males are called *bulls* or *steers*. Together they are called *cattle*.

Herefords are a popular breed of beef cattle. They are rusty brown with white faces.

Ii

Ice Cold Ice Cream

frosty, creamy, smooth, and sweet, ice cream is my favorite treat!

feel the icy ice cream tingle your tongue, just like fresh snowflakes. So good and so simple, ice cream is made by mixing milk or cream with flavors and sweeteners and then slowly cooling it down till it freezes. Vanilla, chocolate, strawberry, cookies and cream, pumpkin pie—**what's your favorite flavor?**

Do you want to have strong bones and muscles? Drink lots of milk. It's full of calcium and protein.

Can you name some other foods we make from milk?

Jj

Juggling Jiggly Jams and Jellies

It's fall harvest! Time for munching sweet, juicy apples, jumping into leaf piles, and carving jolly jack-o'-lanterns. Every fall, pumpkin growers bring their giants to fall fairs to try to win the top prize. The biggest pumpkin so far was grown in Ohio and **weighed over 1,700 pounds.**

JELLY JELLY JELLY JELLY JELLY JELLY

JAM JAM JAM JAM JAM JAM

Jolly orchards farm stand
Homemade
Jams and Jellies
For sale

KK | King-sized Kohlrabi

Is that an octopus in the garden?

No, it's a vegetable! Kohlrabi are sweet-tasting bulbs with thick stems that grow above the ground. While they're usually about the size of a tennis ball, some—like the king-sized Kossak kohlrabi—can grow as big as a volleyball.

Some varieties of watermelons, squashes, cabbages, peppers, and pumpkins can also grow into giants. But even the biggest pumpkin starts life as a tiny seed. Imagine a pumpkin as big as a giant tortoise—that's the granddaddy of all vegetables, the Atlantic Giant pumpkin.

Farmer-friendly bugs that prey on plant-eating pests: Ladybugs • Big-Eyed Bugs •

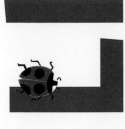

Ladybug's Lunch

Look out APHIDS! Here comes a ladybug and she's hungry.

Ladybugs are always hungry and will spend all day munching on their favorite snack: juicy green aphids. During her lifetime of about one year, one little ladybug may eat as many as five-thousand aphids. No wonder farmers love ladybugs and use them as a natural way to keep aphids from harming their crops!

How many ladybugs can you spot in this picture?

Ladybug Lore

- Ladybugs, also called *ladybirds*, are a type of beetle.
- Not all ladybugs are **ladies**. Some are **lads**.
- Most ladybugs are red or orange with black spots, but some have no spots at all.
- When ladybugs are threatened, they produce a bad-smelling chemical that keeps predators away.
- Ladybugs don't fly at night.
- Ladybugs hibernate during the winter.

Praying Mantis • Hover Flies • Green Lacewings • Spiders • Soldier Beetles • Damsel Bugs

Mm

Making Merry in the Mud and Muck

"I love to wallow in the mud," declares the pig. He kicks up his hooves and wiggles onto his back to get a nice coating of mud on his sensitive pink skin. He knows the mud will keep him cool and protect him from insect bites and sunburn.

"Why are we so misunderstood?" his brother pig huffs as he wallows in the soft, goopy muck. "People actually think we're dirty."

"That's rubbish," replies the first pig. "We are clean animals! I can't stand it when my sty or bed is dirty. Unlike some of those other animals in the barn, I make my manure pile as far away as possible from where I sleep and eat."

"Absolutely," his brother agrees.

"Never mind," the first pig exclaims as he pounces in the muck. "We have better things to do than wonder what humans think about pigs."

Big Bill, who was from Jackson, Tennessee, holds the world record for largest pig. He weighed over 2,500 pounds and was over nine feet long!

Nn

Nibbling Nectar

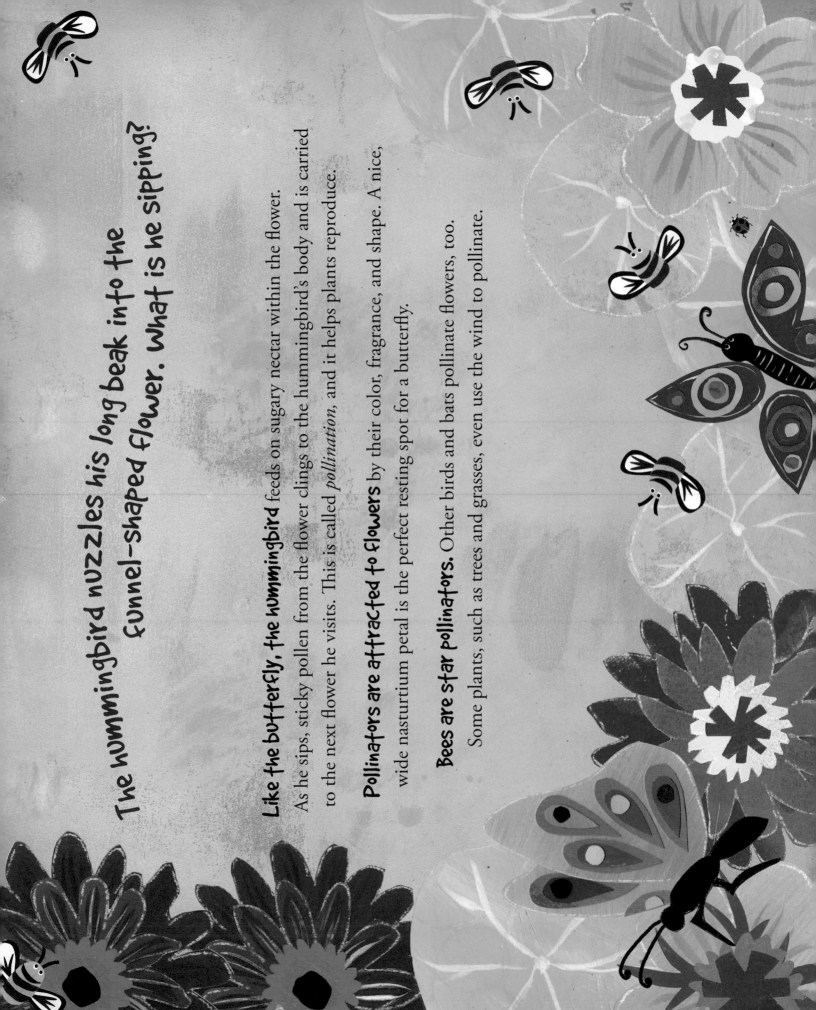

The hummingbird nuzzles his long beak into the funnel-shaped flower. What is he sipping?

Like the butterfly, the hummingbird feeds on sugary nectar within the flower. As he sips, sticky pollen from the flower clings to the hummingbird's body and is carried to the next flower he visits. This is called *pollination*, and it helps plants reproduce.

Pollinators are attracted to flowers by their color, fragrance, and shape. A nice, wide nasturtium petal is the perfect resting spot for a butterfly.

Bees are star pollinators. Other birds and bats pollinate flowers, too. Some plants, such as trees and grasses, even use the wind to pollinate.

Oo

Oh! Overalls in the Orchard

The farmer's trees are full of fruit.
The apples are ripe and ready to pick.

Planting fruit trees together, in groups called orchards, makes it easier to care for them and harvest their fruit. Some apple trees can grow to be over forty feet tall, but most apple growers trim their trees so that ladders will reach the top. While many fruits and vegetables are machine harvested, every apple is picked by hand.

Many fruits such as apples, peaches, pears, and plums grow on trees. Can you think of any others?

Way up high
in an apple tree
Two red apples
smiled at me.
I shook that tree
as hard as I could.
Down came the apples
and m-m-m
they were good.

Pp

Pea Pods Pop!

Five little peas
In a pea pod pressed.
One grew,
Two grew,
And so did all the rest.
They grew and grew,
And did not stop,
Until one day the pod went

PoP!

Snow pea · Sugar Lace · Sugar Sprint · Sugar Ann · Little Marvel · Tall Telephone · Sweet Snap

Qq

The Queen's Quivering Hive

The hive quivers as the queen's workers arrive.

The queen is the largest bee and is the mother of all the bees in the colony. In the spring she lays eggs day and night. As soon as they are born, her daughters, called *worker bees*, are her helpers and will feed and look after the larvae. At two weeks old, worker bees are able to leave the nest to gather sugary water, called *nectar*, that is produced by flowers. Each bee visits hundreds of flowers, drinking up nectar and storing it in her special stomach called a *honey stomach*. The honey stomach is a nectar backpack, and when it is full, the bee returns to the hive and passes the nectar on to a hive bee.

It's buzzing inside the hive as hive bees fan the liquid nectar with their wings to dry it. When the honey is ready, they store it in hexagon-shaped cells so the hive has food during the winter months.

The beekeeper does his job quietly and quickly so as not to disturb the bees. His bee farm, called an *apiary* (a-pee-air-ee), provides a place for the colony to live. The beekeeper harvests only the extra honey, leaving plenty for the bees to eat through the winter when plants are not in flower.

Only female bees have stingers. They use these to guard the hive and protect their queen.

Rr

Reliable Red Rooster

The rooster rises with the sun every day on the farm. What a racket he makes!

The rooster doesn't just crow in the morning. He will crow at any time of day, all day long. That's because a rooster crows to let the hens know when he's found something good to eat or to warn them of trouble in the barnyard. He will also crow to let other roosters in the neighborhood know who's in charge.

Hens are quieter. They cluck when they are startled or when they have laid an egg.

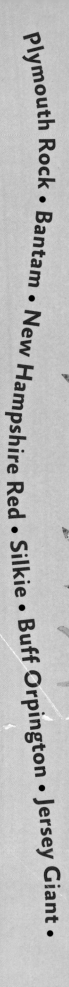

Plymouth Rock • Bantam • New Hampshire Red • Silkie • Buff Orpington • Jersey Giant •

Five Fowl Facts

1. The chicken is the closest living relative to the Tyrannosaurus Rex.

2. Chickens don't have teeth, and their beaks don't do the chewing—their gizzards do. The gizzard is a muscular pouch in the chicken's stomach that uses the grit and gravel the chicken has swallowed to help grind up hard foods like grain.

3. There are more chickens than people in the world.

4. If there is no rooster in a flock, a hen will take over, stop laying eggs, and start crowing.

5. A chicken can run up to nine miles per hour.

COCK-A-DOODLE-DOO!

Wh...e...horn • Rosecomb • Silver Cuckoo • Rhode Island Red

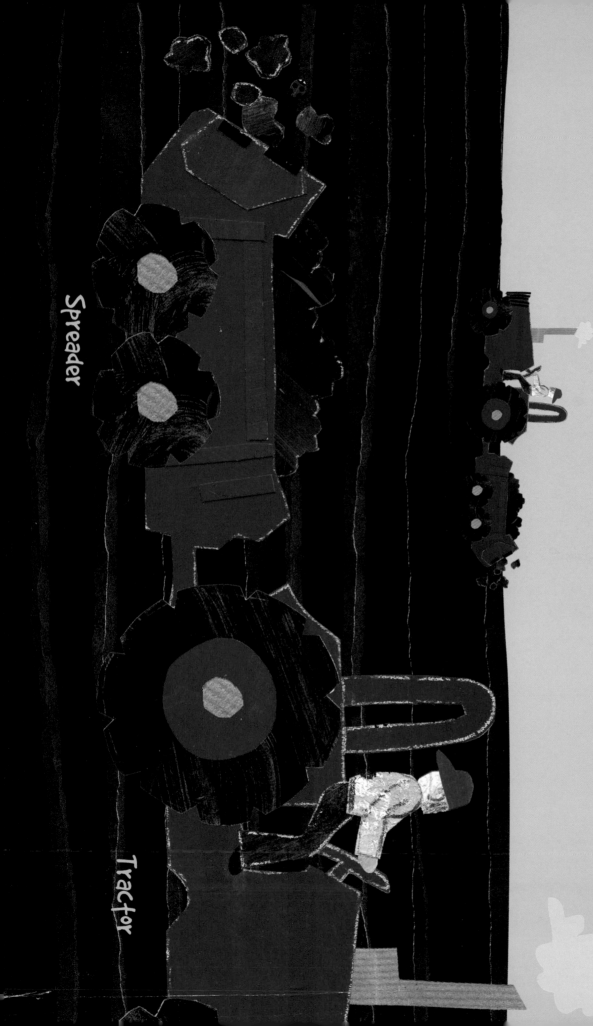

Ss

Stink, Stank, Stunk

Spreader

Tractor

The farmer uses a spreader to spread manure on her fields. It stinks! But to the farmer it's a good smell. Manure is food for her soil and her crops.

Seeder

Soil has a secret ingredient called humus. Humus is rich, dark earth made from rotting vegetables and animal waste. At home, we put food scraps in our compost pile to make humus for our garden. The farmer takes manure from her animals and piles it up to make a huge compost heap.

Worms, insects, snails, and small rodents help out by creating tunnels that allow air to enter and decompose the pile. The farmer adds the nutrient-rich composted manure to the soil to help her crops grow.

The smallest earthworms are less than half an inch, and the largest can be over thirteen feet long. That's longer than a tractor!

Tt

Tip Top Tasty Tomato

It's an easy life for hothouse tomatoes. They have everything they need inside their toasty glass houses: just the right amount of water, the perfect temperature, and protection from pesky insects. In a warm greenhouse, a tomato can even grow in the middle of winter. It's like summer all year long!

Is a tomato a fruit or a vegetable? A vegetable is the edible stem, leaves, or roots of a plant. A fruit is the edible part of the plant that contains the seeds. Since we eat the part with the seeds, a tomato is a fruit.

These tomato plants like it so much in their greenhouse that they may grow up to thirty feet long.

Guess which of these tomatoes is used to make ketchup? Goliath • Burpee • Super Steak •

I'm a Big Red Tomato

I'm a Big Red Tomato
Growing on a vine,
A big red tomato
Looking on, so fine.
Now you can make good things with me—
Soup, juice, pizza, to name just three.
I'm a big red tomato
Growing on a vine.
Grow, grow, grow.

Small Fry • Red Robin • Tiny Tim • Banana Legs • Bonny Best • Taxi • Heinz

Uu

Udders Under Umbrellas

Everyone wakes up early for first milking, even on rainy days.

Twice a day, in the morning and the evening, the dairy cow follows the farmer to the milking barn to give him her milk. Like the other black-and-white spotted cows on this dairy farm, she's a Holstein. The farmer tells his Holsteins apart by their spots. Just like our fingerprints, each cow's pattern of spots is unique to her alone.

The farmer feeds his dairy cows a mixture of hay and grain.

The cow uses the energy from her feed to make milk for her calf. One Holstein can make enough milk every day to fill almost one hundred glasses of milk. That's more than her calf needs, so there's some left over for the farmer.

Making milk is thirsty work.
A dairy cow will drink about a bathtub full of water every day.

Vv

Vegetable Voyage

Have you ever wondered what vegetables would
talk about if they could speak?

"Are we there yet?" the broccolini whined for the tenth time.

"Better be soon," the tomato replied. "One more bump and I'll be bruised for sure!"

"I don't know what you're fussing about," moaned the lettuce.

"What if my leaves wilt in this heat?"

"But it's cold and drafty outside!" complained the mini-cucumbers. "We liked it better in the greenhouse."

"We're thirsty!" the baby carrots all cried together.

"Wait a minute!" bellowed the cabbage. "Quit your bellyaching. You've all been grown just for this journey. We'll be at the farmers' market before you know it, so sit back and enjoy the ride."

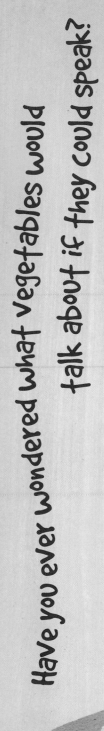

Woolly Bears
Worry Watermelons

Woolly bear caterpillars come in lots of colors, but most are black on both ends with an orange stripe in the middle. The best time to find one is in the fall when they are crawling about in search of a sheltered space to spend the winter. But first, fill the bottom of a plastic container with a damp cloth and some dry leaves. Poke a few airholes in the lid so your woolly bear can breathe. Now gently put your woolly bear in his new winter home, and keep it in a cold place like the balcony or porch. Let your bear sleep.

In the spring your bear will wake up hungry, so find him some fresh dandelions (his favorite food) and damp soil. After feeding a bit, he will spin his silk cocoon and pupate. Now wait for almost two weeks, and then a tiger moth will magically emerge. That's called *metamorphosis* (met-ah-mor-fuh-siss). Release your moth that night so it can return to nature and repeat the life cycle.

Is that a moth or a butterfly? Does it have a furry body with feathery antennae? Then it's a moth. If it has knobs at the ends of its antennae, it's a butterfly.

Do you think the watermelon is worried
that the waltzing woolly bears might fall off?

Xx/Yy

Xtra-large Eggs with Yummy Yellow Yolks

Chickens come in different sizes and so do their eggs. The smallest eggs are called Peewees, and the large are called Jumbo and Extra-large.

Most of the eggs we eat come from chickens called "layers." Duck, geese, and quail are raised for their eggs, too. Of course, ostriches lay the largest eggs. Eating one ostrich egg is the same as eating almost twenty-four chicken eggs. **That's one big fried egg!**

Can you guess the name of the mixed chicken breed that lays green or blue eggs?

Easter Eggers of course!

What happens when you tell an egg a joke? It cracks up.

The most yolks ever found in one egg was

Most chickens lay brownish eggs, sometimes with a pink, red, orange, or lavender hue—some are even speckled. Rhode Island Red hens lay glossy brown eggs. A Plymouth Rock lays dark pink eggs. A Yokohama is a white chicken with an elegant long tail and lays cream-colored eggs. And, Cuckoo Marans are sometimes called Chocolate Eggers for the deep chocolate-brown eggs they lay.

A fun way to find out if a hen lays colored eggs is to check her ears! Gently push aside the feathers just below the chicken's eyes toward the back of her head, and check the flap of skin on her small ear opening. Hens with red or pink ears lay colored eggs and pale-eared hens lay white eggs.

Chickens that eat lots of green plants and bugs lay eggs with bright yellow yolks. These are the yummiest.

Did you know that hens don't need a rooster to lay eggs? The rooster is only needed to fertilize the eggs and produce chicks.

Have you ever seen a zucchini race? Let's turn the page. . . .

Zz

Zoom Zoom Zucchini

The zucchini are ripe and raring to go—time for the annual zucchini race! Line your car up at the top of the plank, wait for the start and . . . they're off!

Our Zucchini Race Rules:

1. Use any size zucchini. Bigger is not always faster.
2. Give it four wheels. Toy car or skateboard wheels are great.
3. Gravity-powered only. No motors allowed!
4. Decorate your zucchini to give it extra pizzazz.
5. When the race is over don't forget to eat your zucchini or put it in your compost pile!

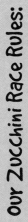

Can you find these words and

one little ladybug has hidden herself in each illustration in this book. See if you can spot her!

images in this edible alphabet?

For Sebastian, Julia, Kayla, and Brenna—our number one readers and vegetable eaters. —Carol & Michela

Text copyright © 2011 by Carol Watterson
Illustrations copyright © 2011 by Michela Sorrentino

Tricycle Press and the Tricycle Press colophon are registered trademarks of Random House, Inc.

Originally published in 2009 in Canada as *Alfalfabet A to Z, The Wonderful Words from
Agriculture* by the British Columbia Agriculture in the Classroom Foundation.

"The Apple Tree," "Five Little Peas," and "I'm a Big Red Tomato" by authors unknown.

Library of Congress Cataloging-in-Publication Data

Watterson, Carol.
An edible alphabet : 26 reasons to love the farm / by Carol Watterson;
illustrated by Michela Sorrentino.
        p. cm.
1. Farms—Juvenile literature. 2. Food crops—Juvenile literature.
3. Farm animals—Juvenile literature. 4. English language—Alphabet.
I. Sorrentino, Michela, ill. II. Title.
S519.W38 2011
530—dc22

                                        2010030478

ISBN 978-1-58246-421-3 (hardcover)
ISBN 978-1-58246-422-0 (Gibraltar lib. bdg.)

Printed in China

Interior design by Betsy Stromberg and Michela Sorrentino
Jacket/Cover design by Betsy Stromberg
Typeset in Adobe Garamond Pro and Good Dog Plain
The illustrations in this book were prepared using collage
with handpainted papers and acrylics.

1 2 3 4 5 6 – 16 15 14 13 12 11

First Edition